Wonderland

Preface

There obviously is no Wonderland without a certain loss of control.
Alice is lost in Wonderland. Fairytales help children make the transition
from the state of wakefulness into the uncertain territory of dreams
– both good and bad. The human (and obviously the animal) brain
repeats the experiences and emotional states of the day while the body
rests. At night brain cells draw new connections and create new neural
patterns that help the brain to remember and to learn. New paths are
being paved from the once experienced through and into uncharted
territory. The words "wonder" and "wound" come from the same origin
and "amazement" means that you are in a maze. Whatever touches
us has the power to hurt us. Whatever seems real lives a second more
unbalanced identity in Wonderland.

While romance (Romantik) is a projection – a longing for a wider,
more spectacular existence – Wonderland is intense experience, a reverie,
a quick or maybe a long stay in a rapidly changing surrounding. A lot
of the illustrations and photography featured in this book try to reflect
this intensity; there is little quietness in the works. Wonderland's
ornaments are not static; they are liquid. Everything seems to be caught
in a fragile moment and even the stills are fantastic – woods are wicked
and skies ablaze. The fascination finally sets in with the return of
the "traveller". The shiver of having encountered the unknown and
returning without a scratch makes a person feel alive. And isn't this
what most people hunger for?

Linn Olofsdotter Costa

Linn Olofsdotter Costa

Container

Linn Olofsdotter Costa

Sunday Vision

Marco Cibola

Marco Cibola

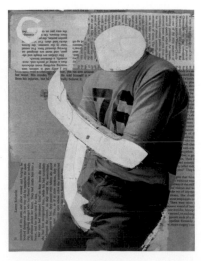

James Gallager

James Gallager

James Gallager

Nawel

livre vivre

Linn Olofsdotter Costa

Mikko Rantanen

Speto

For Paul Mauriat

Toshifumi Tanabu

Taobot | Danny Franzreb

digitally mastered

Taobot | Danny Franzreb

ORINE.

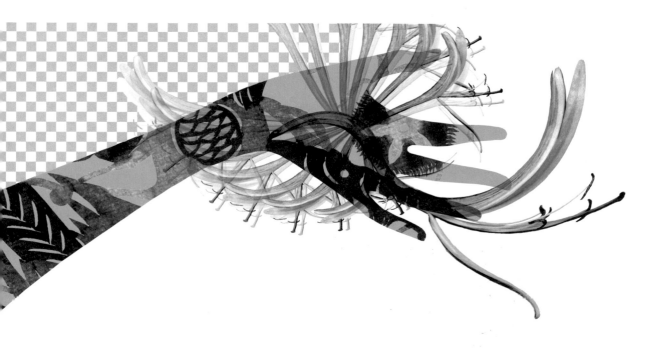

Matte

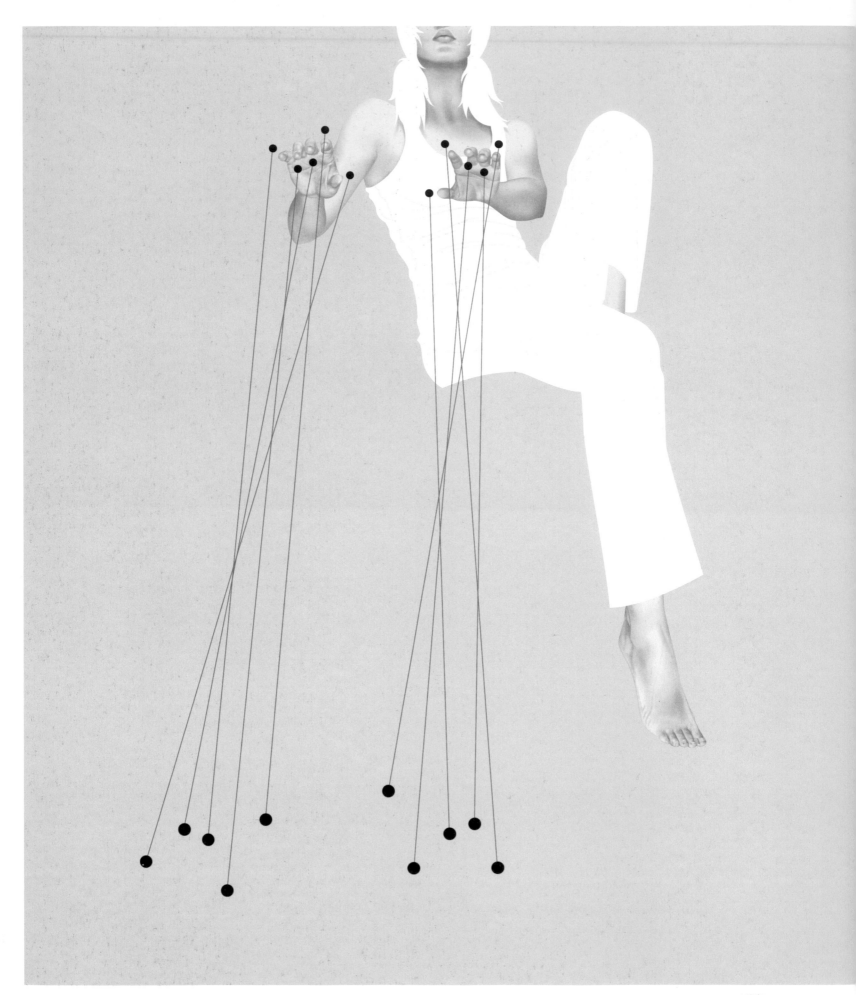

Autumn Whitehurst

Autumn Whitehurst

Cecilia Carlstedt

Cecilia Carlstedt

Cecilia Carlstedt

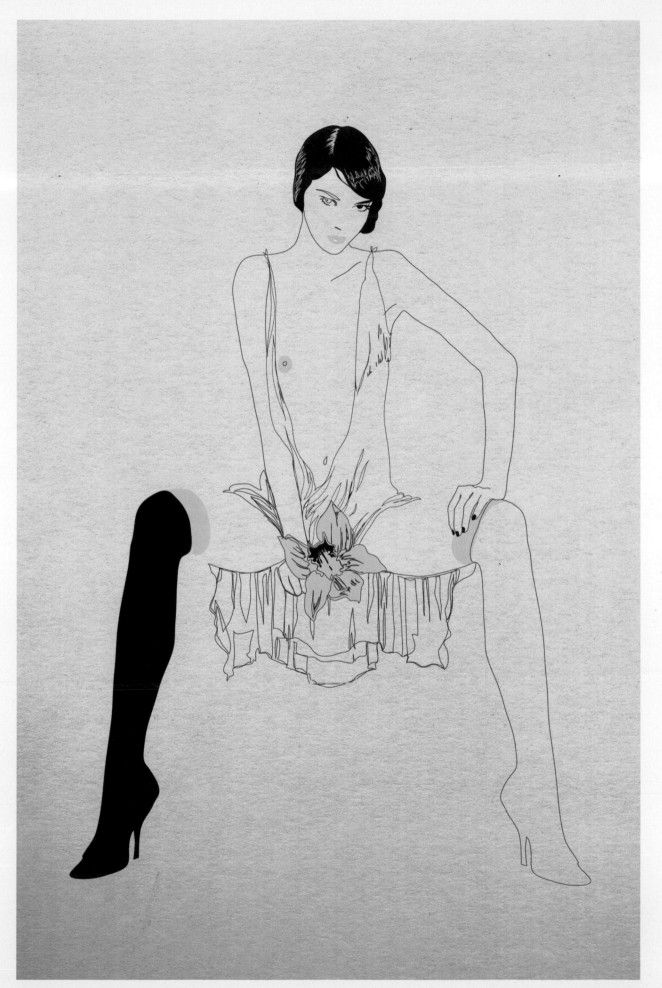

Cecilia Carlstedt

olofsdotter

Linn Olofsdotter Costa

Kareem İliya

ITA DIIS PLACUIT

SUPERMODEL
CITIZEN
OF
THE
NATION
OF
ANGELA

NOLI ME TANGERE

SUPERMODEL
CITIZEN
OF
THE
NATION
OF
ANGELA

Sophie Toulouse

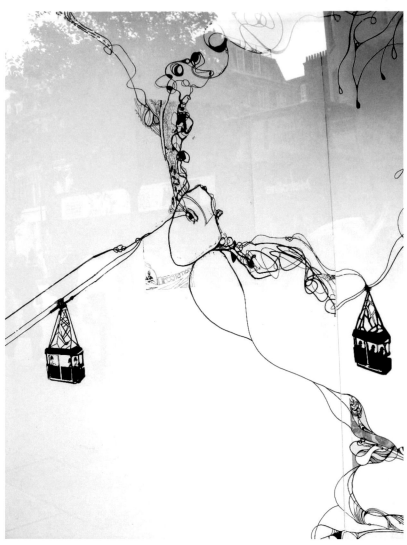

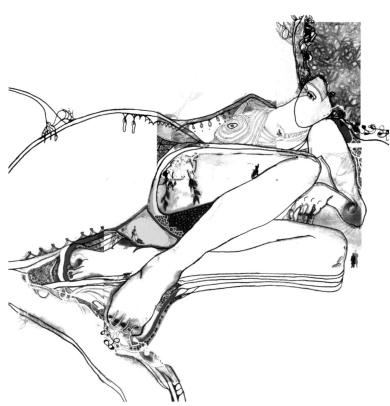

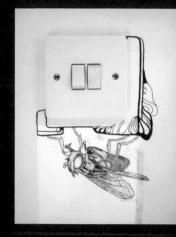

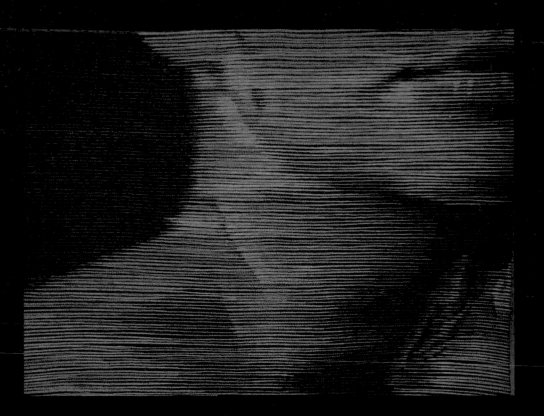

Inga Liksaite

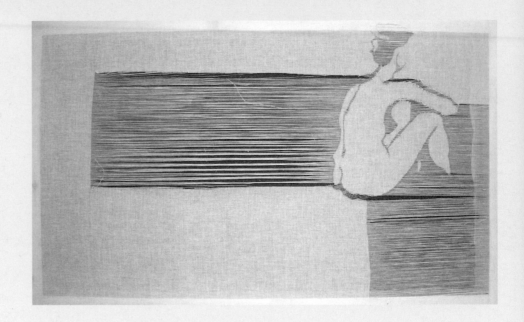

Ngo Phuc Hien

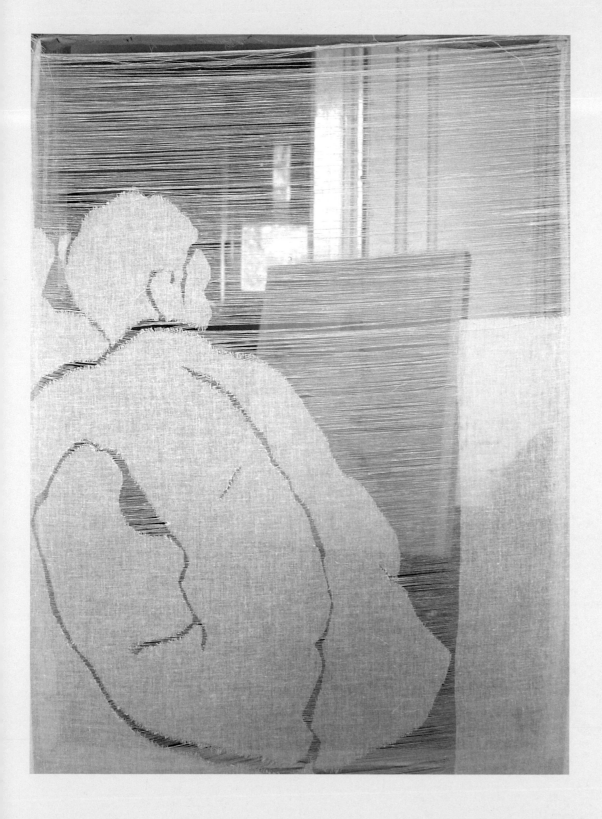

69

Ngo Phuc Hien

Kiyoshi Kuroda

70

Kiyoshi Kuroda

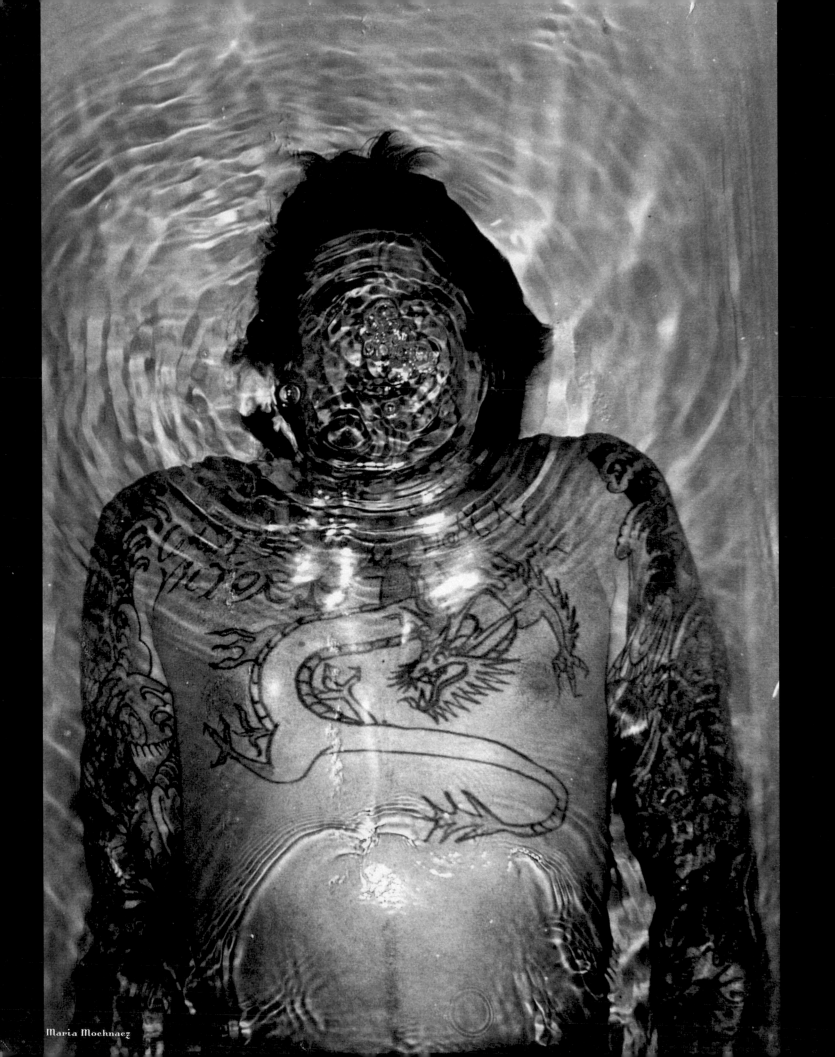

Maria Mochnacz

Ìnocuo Design

Won Ju Lim

Won Ju Lim

Won Ju Lim

Mikko Rantanen

Mikko Rantanen

Erwin Olaf

Koen Hauser

Koen Hauser

Koen Hauser

Txema Yeste

Txema Yeste

Txema Yeste

Maren Esdar

Maren Esdar

Maren Esdar

Maren Esdar

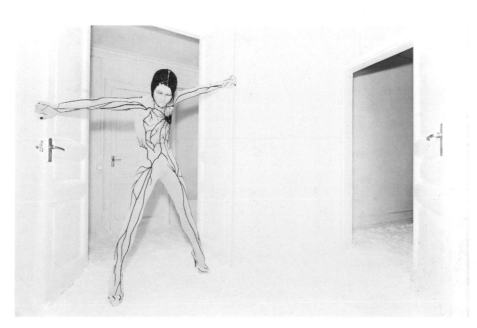

Txema Yeste

Richard Gray

107   Richard Gray

Richard Gray

Richard Gray

Simen Johan

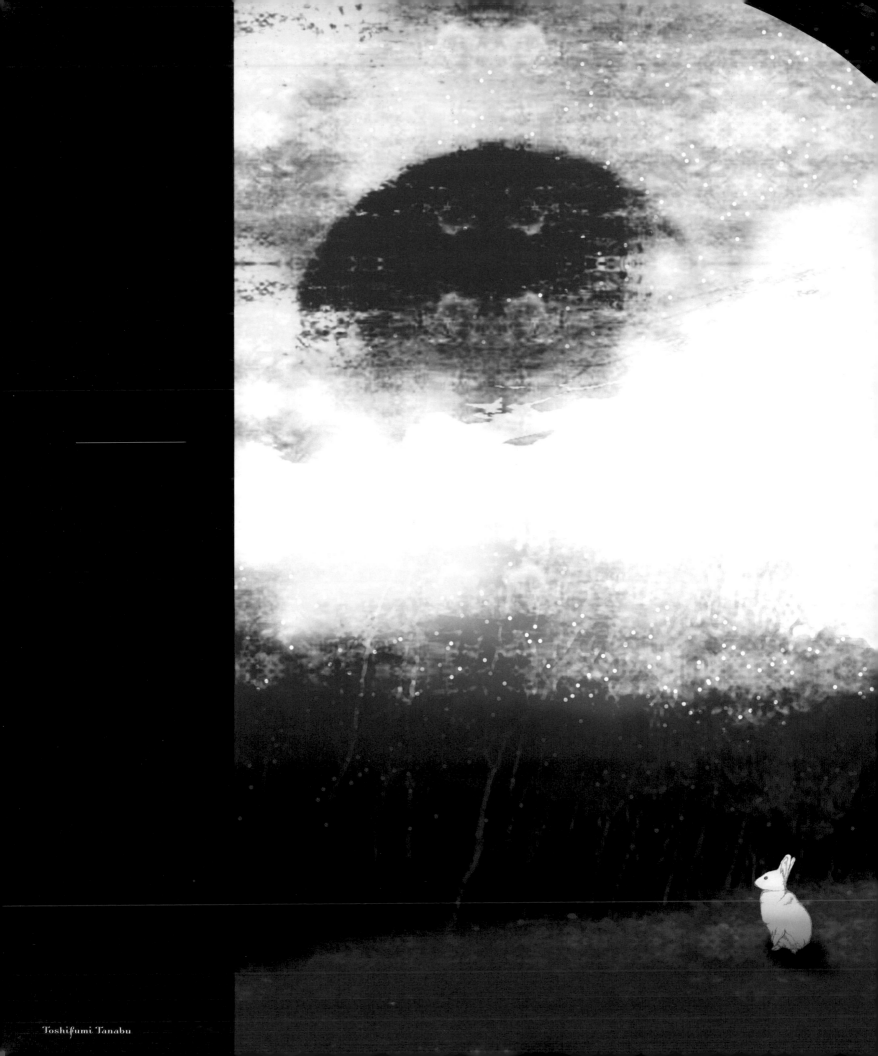

Toshifumi Tanabu

Thomas Barwick

Greyscale

Toshifumi Tanabu

Toshifumi Tanabu

Toshifumi Tanabu

Erwin Olaf

Liselotte Watkins

Liselotte Watkins

Liselotte Watkins

Liselotte Watkins

Vault49.com

◇ = collaboration with Katja Mayer

✈ = collaboration with Stephan Langmanis

Pandarosa

Sei Hishikawa

Toshifumi Tanabu

Toshifumi Tanabu

Toshifumi Tanabu

GOLD
BLATT

Pandarosa

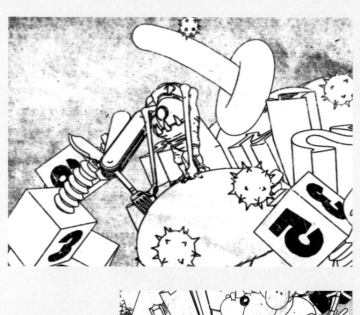

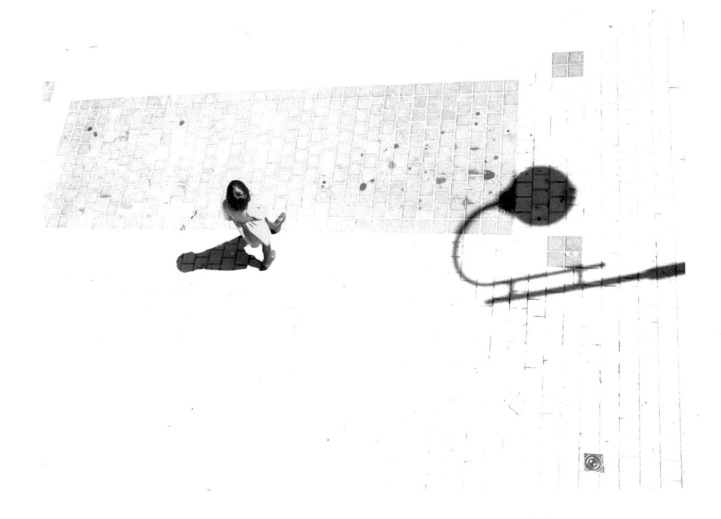

Index

Lobo
Brazil
www.lobo.cx
info@lobo.cx

Page 154, 155

Matte
Amsterdam - The Netherlands
www.matte.nl
info@matte.nl

Page 43: for online fashion
magazine JC Report
(www.jcreport.com)

Craig Metzger
New York - USA
www.enginesystem.com
craig@enginesystem.com

Page 156

mijuly
Berlin - Germany
mijuly@gmx.de

Page 65 (top): "Lucy", 2004,
72 x 130 cm; "Aphrodite" 1&2,
2004, 53 x 140 cm und 76 x 140
cm; "Lollita", 2004, 94 x 124 cm
Page 65 (bottom): "Madame" I-IV,
2004, 70,4 x 140 cm each
Images taken at the Rosengarten
Gallery in Berlin, Germany
Photography Stephan Rabold
(www.stephan-rabold.com)

Maria Mochnacz
London - UK

Represented by
Kloss Management
London - UK
www.klosslondon.com
info@klosslondon.com

Page 72, 73

Nawel
Paris - France

Represented by Unit CMA
Amsterdam - The Netherlands
www.unit.nl
info@unit.nl

Page 30, 31

Erwin Olaf
Amsterdam - The Netherlands
www.erwinolaf.com
info@erwinolaf.com

Page 88 - 90
Page 128 - 133

Linn Olofsdotter Costa
Boston - USA
www.olofsdotter.com
linn@olofsdotter.com

Page 4, 5
Page 10, 11
Page 32, 33
Page 52, 53

Pandarosa
Melbourne - Australia
www.pandarosa.net
info@pandarosa.net

Page 59
Page 64
Page 146
Page 152, 153

Mikko Rantanen
London - UK
www.mikkorantanen.com
mikko-rantanen@jippii.fi

Page 34, 35
Page 82 - 87

Sophy Rickett
London - UK

Represented by
Emily Tsingou Gallery
London - UK
www.emilytsingougallery.com
emily@emilytsingougallery.com

Page 76 (top): "Via di Bravetta 2",
2002; 100 x 100 cm each;
2 C-print mounted on aluminum
Page 76 (bottom): "Cypress Screen,
Dundee", 2001; 100 x 100 cm
each, 3 Black and white photo-
graphs mounted on aluminum

Speto
Sao Paolo - Brazil
www.speto.com
speto@speto.com

Page 36, 37
Page 63

Toshifumi Tanabu
Tokyo - Japan
www.geocities.jp/t_tanabu
t_tanabu@ybb.ne.jp

Page 39
Page 120, 121
Page 125 - 127
Page 148 - 151

Taobot / Danny Franzreb
Frankfurt am Main - Germany
www.taobot.com
danny@taobot.com

Page 40, 41

Sophie Toulouse
Paris - France
www.sophietoulouse.com
nationofangela@mac.com

Page 56 - 58

Vault 49
New York - USA
www.vault49.com
info@vault49.com

Page 44: Photography by Stephan
Langmanis
Page 45
Page 140 - 143: Photography by
Stephan Langmanis
Page 144, 145: Photography by
Katja Mayer

Sunday Vision
Tokyo - Japan
www.sunday-vision.com
info@sunday-vision.com

Page 12
Page 13: Piece of Peace LEGO
Exhibition
Page 14: Casa BRUTUS cover
artwork
Page 15
Page 17: BEAMS T, DISTRACT.
with FJD
Page 38: Silver Spoon
Page 42: ORINE. 2003
spring/summer catalogue
AD: Atsushi Sato (ORINE.)

Txema Yeste
Barcelona - Spain
www.txyeste.com

Represented by Unit CMA
Amsterdam - The Netherlands
www.unit.nl
info@unit.nl

Page 94 - 97
Page 104, 105

Liselotte Watkins
Stockholm - Sweden

Represented by Agentform
Stockholm - Sweden
www.agentform.com
ebba@agentform.se

Page 134 - 139

Autumn Whitehurst
New York - USA

Represented by Art Department
New York - USA
www.art-dept.com
stephaniep@art-dept.com

Page 46, 47

Wonderland

Edited by Robert Klanten, Sven Ehmann, Birga Meyer

Layout and Design by Birga Meyer
Cover Design by Takeshi Hamada

Preface by Robert Klanten
Translation by Helga Beck
Editorial Support Japan by Junko Hanzawa
Production Management by Janni Milstrey and Vinzenz Geppert

Published by Die Gestalten Verlag, 2004
ISBN 3-89955-067-6

4th Printing 2006

For more information please check:
www.die-gestalten.de

The first edition of Wonderland contains the Diesel Dreams DVD.
We came across some of the projects featured on this disk during
our research and felt it would add value to this book to present the
moving images as well. We hope you appreciate it.
This is no sponsorship! Thanks to Diesel.